The Christmas Star

By Sanja Mach

Illustrator Anastasia Besedina

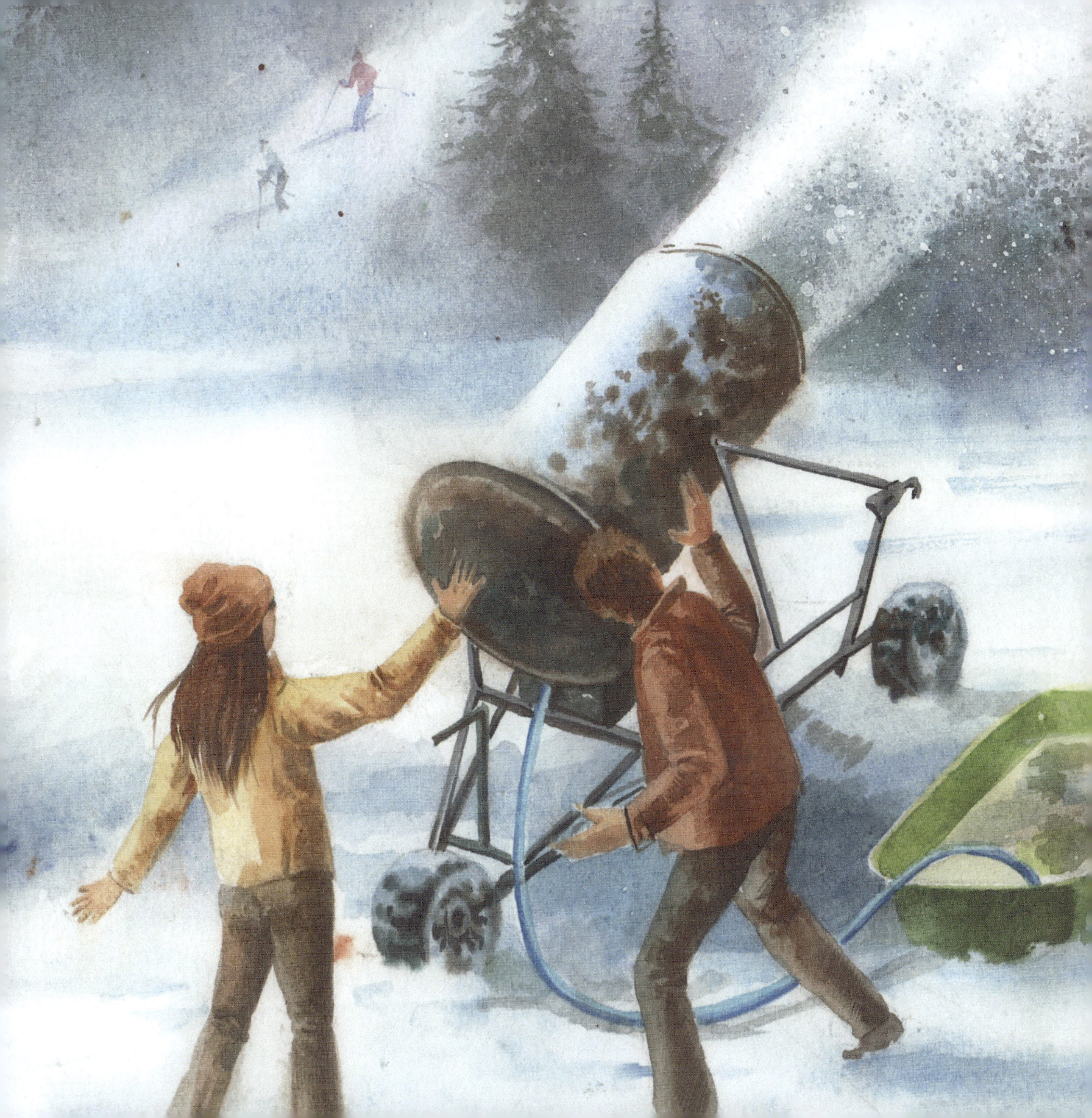

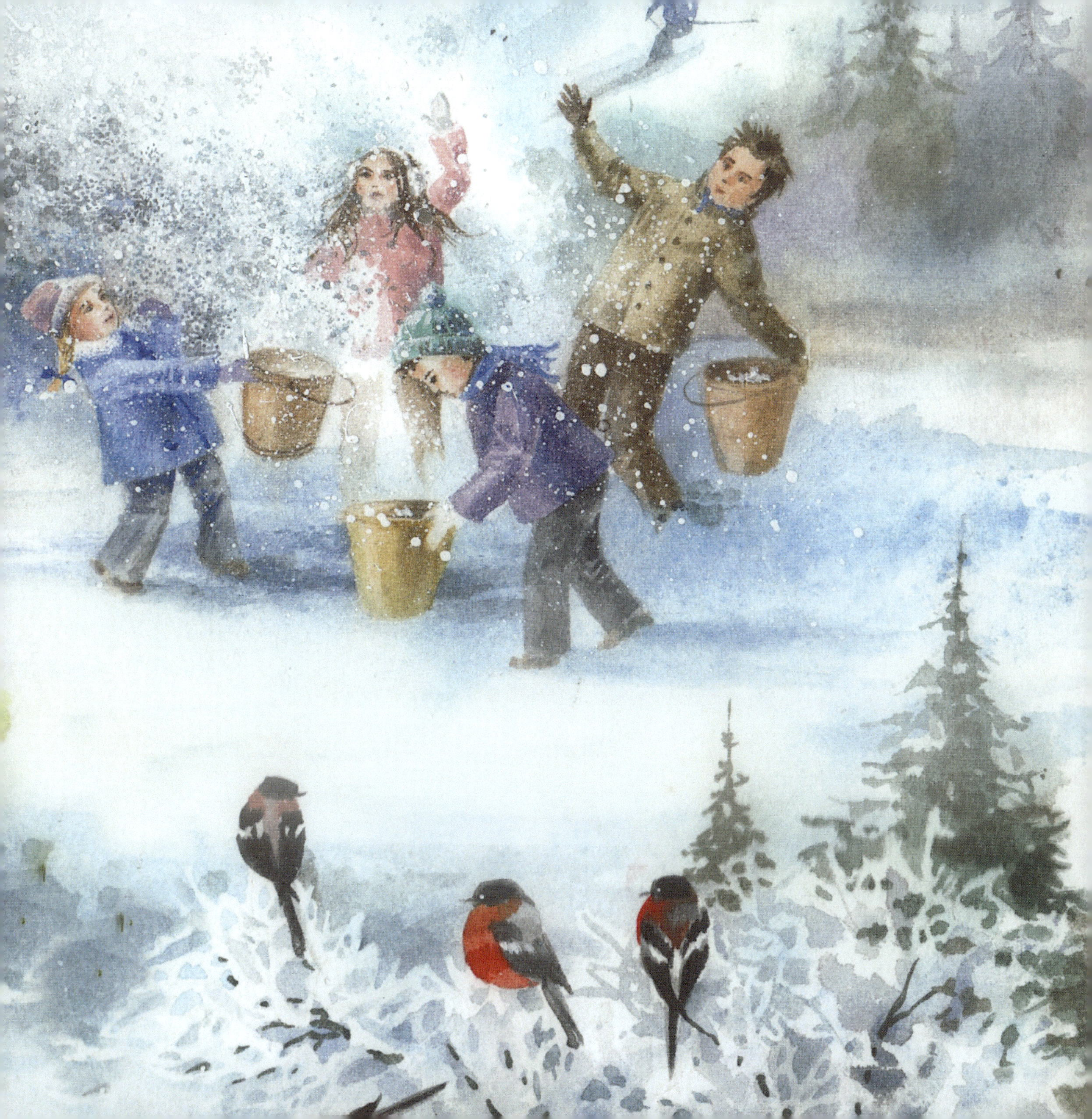

Copyright ©2021 Sanja Mach books
All rights reserved. This book or parts thereof may not be reproduced, photocopied, translated, stored in a database or distributed in any form or by any means (electronic, optical, or mechanical, including photocopying or recording), without the express written and signed consent of the author.

Contact the author at sanjamach@yahoo.com

Language reviewer: Željana Pavlaković

Edited by Calvin Allen

Self – publishing

Print on demand

ISBN 9798946280846

This book belongs to:

The Christmas Star

By Sanja Mach   Illustrator Anastasia Besedina

Split, 2021

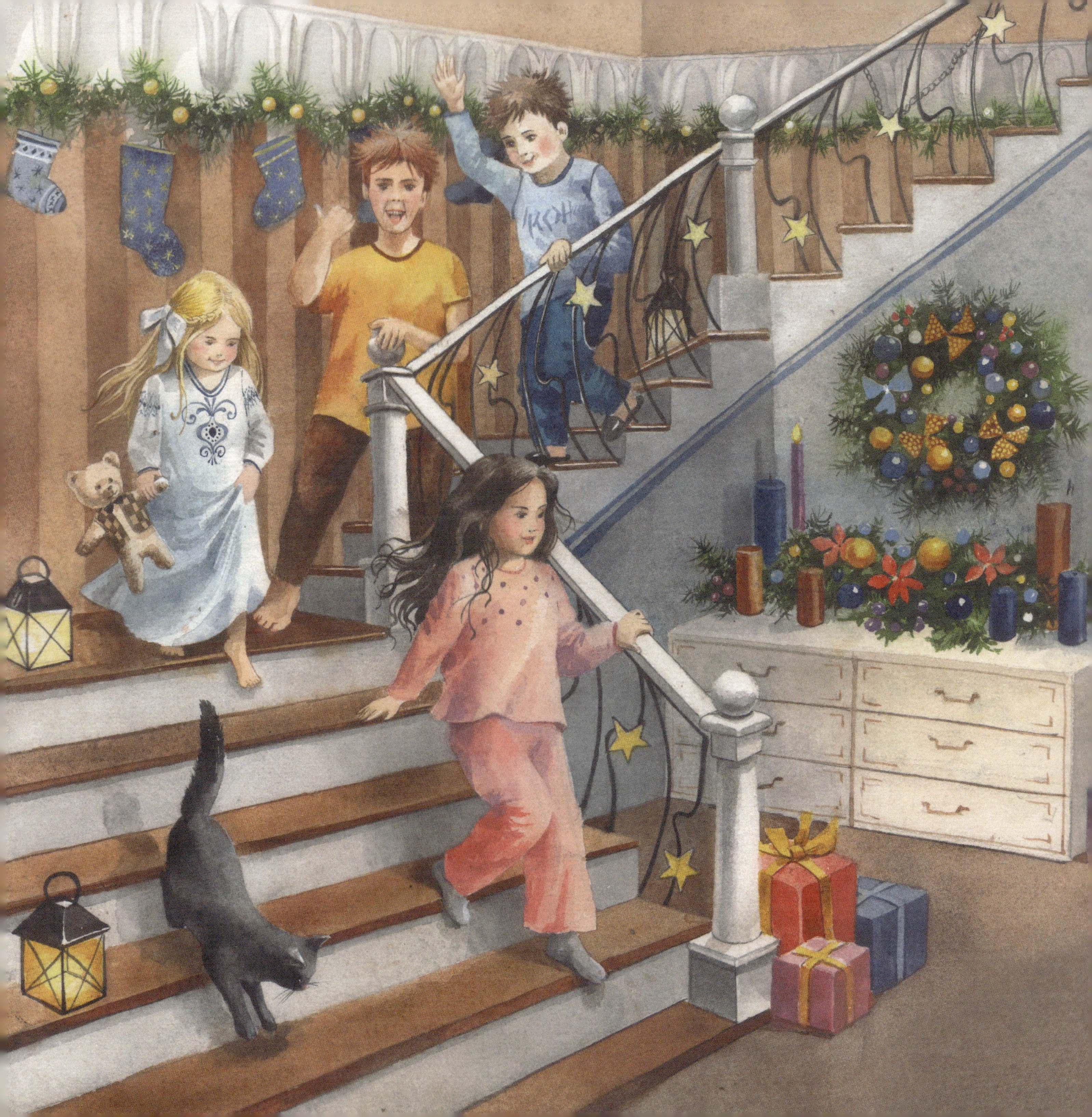

When Mum shouted 'Snow is falling!' at the top of her voice that Christmas Eve morning, all her four lovely children jumped from their warm beds and ran to the closest window in their bedrooms to make sure this was not one of their mother's false wake-up calls. When that didn't provide enough evidence, they all ran down the stairs to see if it was genuinely snowing.

To their delight, so much snow had already fallen that it covered the canopy of nearby trees and the roofs of their neighbours' houses. A white blanket swathed the streets in every direction they could see.

They were all beside themselves with happiness because, in this small mountain village, snow hadn't fallen on this day in four long years.

With their little noses pressed up against the windows, they absorbed every white detail that was no longer in its original shape and colour.

'Let's go outside!' one of them called. 'Not before breakfast!' 'Ohhhh..' they all frowned, simultaneously disapproving of their mother's response.

'Don't be so sad. Wait till you see what I have made you for breakfast!' Mum smiled enigmatically. To their great surprise, Mum had made all their favourites: waffles; doughnuts; and muffins. As if this wasn't enough, she added hot chocolate milk to warm them up.

As soon as they could, they dressed warmly, put on thick gloves and woolly hats and flew outside. At first, they pelted each other with snowballs, then made snow angels and, when they tired of that, finally decided to make a snowman. Holly, the youngest, had been badgering her older sister and her brothers for the whole morning about this and, when the time came, she couldn't stop jumping for joy.

First they made one big ball. Then they put another, smaller, one on top and finally a third, the smallest, for the head. Elizabeth, her older sister, then decided to fetch some large buttons out of a sewing box from inside. 'Can I have the buttons?,' little Holly said to her. After she had arranged them on his face and down his front to do up an imaginary coat, Mum came out of the house and put in place the biggest carrot they had seen for a nose and two black pieces of coal for
the snowman's eyes.

The children didn't have any spare hats, so they put an old metal bucket on his head. A warm blue scarf was lent him by Thomas, Holly's twin brother. Joseph, the tallest of the four, brought perfect twigs for a snowman's hands from the nearby forest. Holly found a spare pair of purple gloves in her coat pockets and she gently pulled them
over his hands.

'Let's have lunch now, and you should warm yourselves up before you all catch cold.' Mum was in a bit of a fuss.

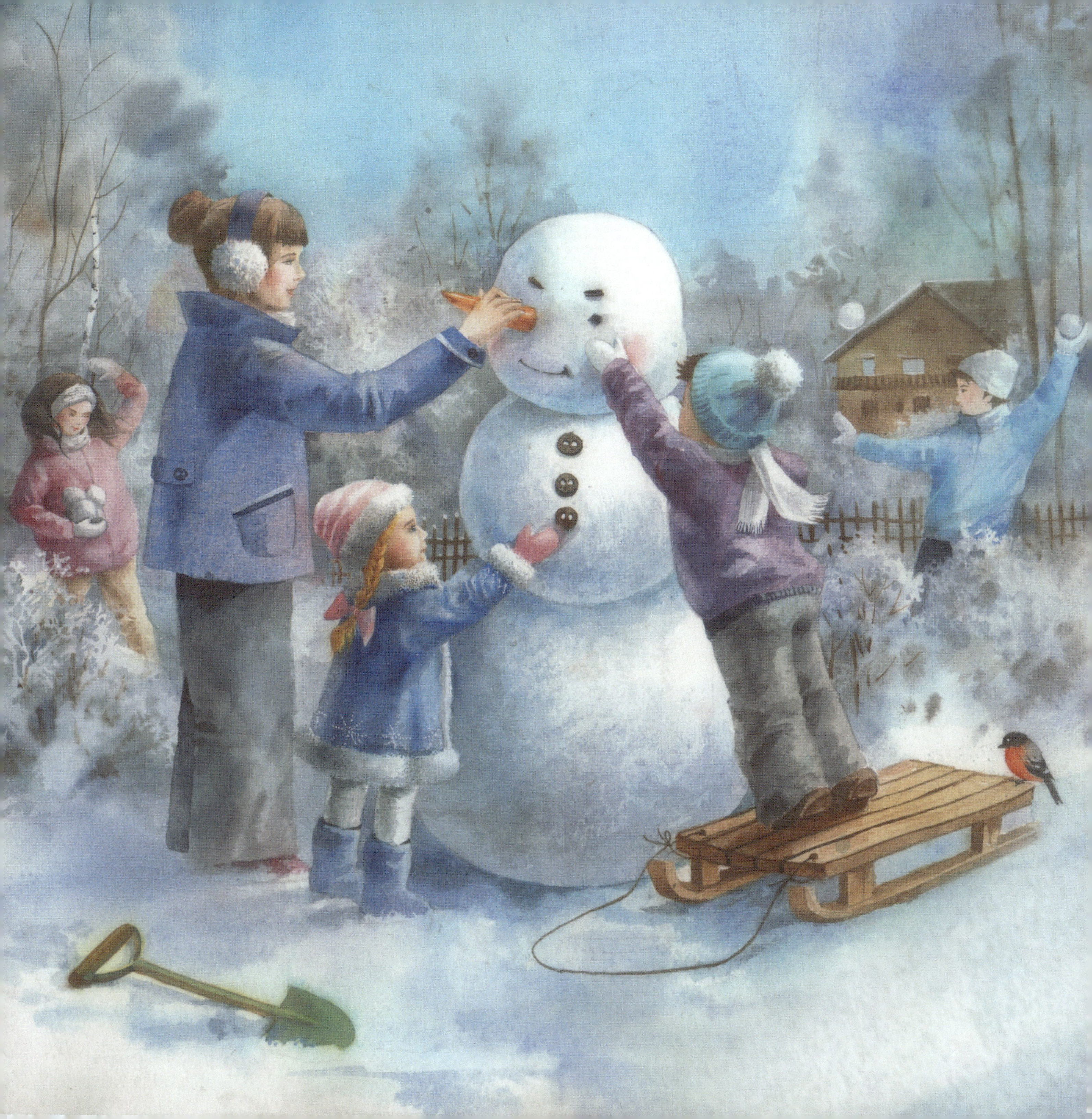

The rest of the day was spent getting ready for the mass that evening but all that was on young Holly's mind was to be outside in the snow. She was so excited about it because, even though they had lived in the mountains ever since she had been born, snow had not fallen at Christmas and to her, like to any child, snow at Christmas was the best thing that
could happen.

'Mum, can I go outside?' Holly asked. 'No sweetheart, it's dark out there now and it's freezing!' 'Please, just for a bit.' 'No, my dear.' 'But, ever since I was born there was no snow, and I want to play in it.' 'The snow will still be here tomorrow and, if you want to play, go upstairs and play with your brothers and sister.' Holly groaned but obeyed, mumbling something to herself while going up the stairs.

Bedtime quickly crept around and, after brushing their teeth, Mum read them a bedtime story. When she was sure that all the other children were asleep, Holly got down from her bunk bed and pressed her nose against the window, hoping to see the snowman. But, instead of him, she saw the Christmas Star above the roofs and trees, shining in the midnight sky.

She held her little palms tightly closed and whispered, 'Dear Christmas Star, for Christmas morning I have only one wish and that is neither a new toy nor a new pencil case. With all my heart I ask you to bring my snowman friend to life.' After finishing her prayer, she climbed into her warm bed, snuggling up to her teddy bear. 'Ah, what a present that would be!' was the one last thought that flew through her mind before she fell sound asleep.

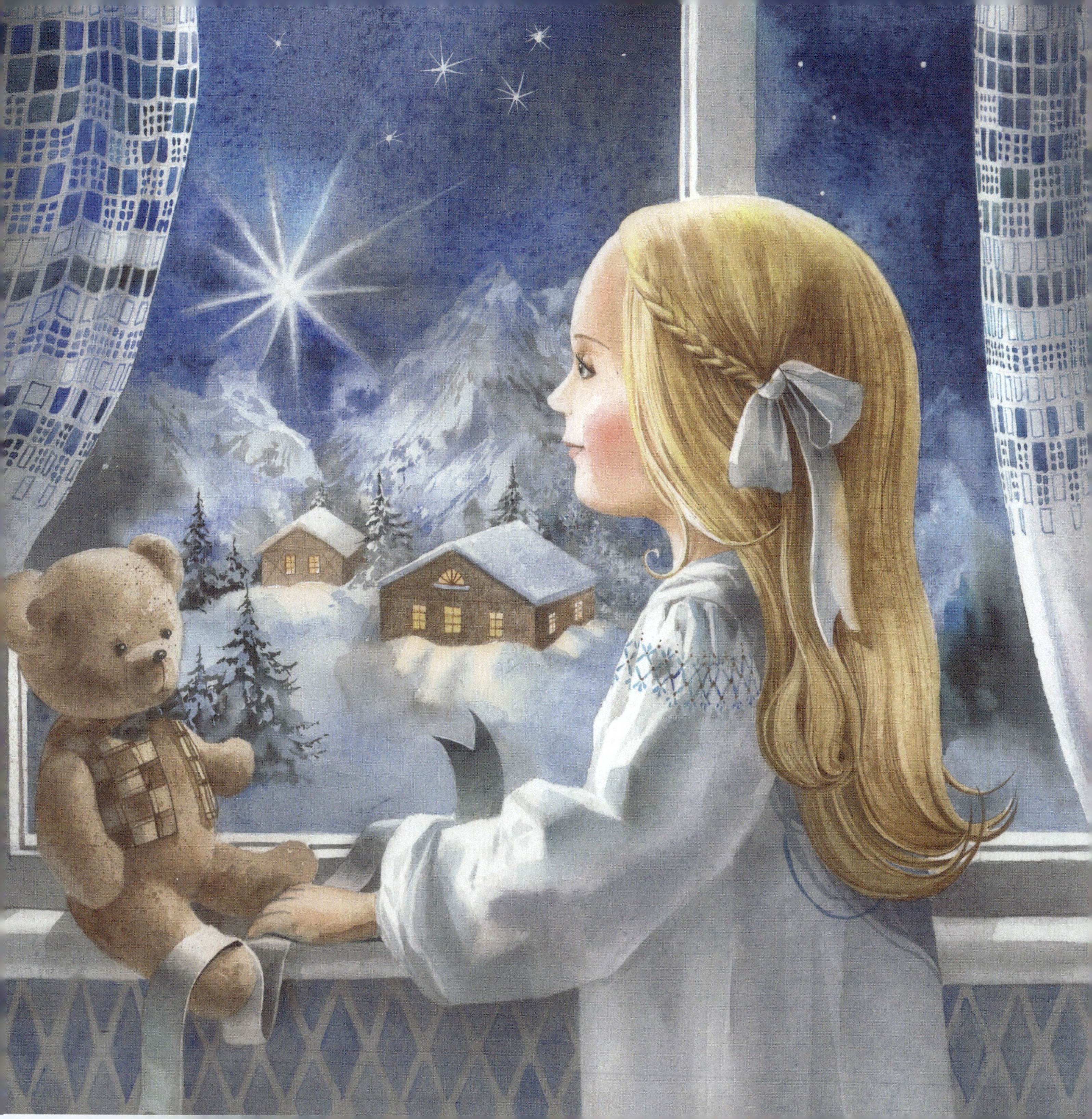

'Hey, where are you running to like this so early in the morning?' Mum asked Holly when she ran into her as she rushed through their home. 'I'm going outside!' 'And what about your presents?' Dad added, confused by Holly's reaction. 'I don't want them,' she said, her confidence spilling over. 'I asked the Christmas Star for the snowman to come alive and I know that she will make it happen!'

Mum and Dad tried to reassure her. When they failed, the rest of the family tried to convince her of the foolishness of her plan, but Holly was persistent. She put on her woolly hat and warm boots, and rushed outside. The others didn't even get the chance to dress, so they just put their coats on.

When they reached the place where the snowman should be, to their surprise there were only two white rabbits and a few small birds greeting them. In the place where the snowman had been the previous day, they found traces in the snow like the prints of a large circle. After a few of these circular prints they glimpsed what looked like one black button; and then, after a few more, another. They all set off, following in the footsteps, not trusting their eyes. To their disbelief, in the woods they spotted him smiling, surrounded by forest creatures.

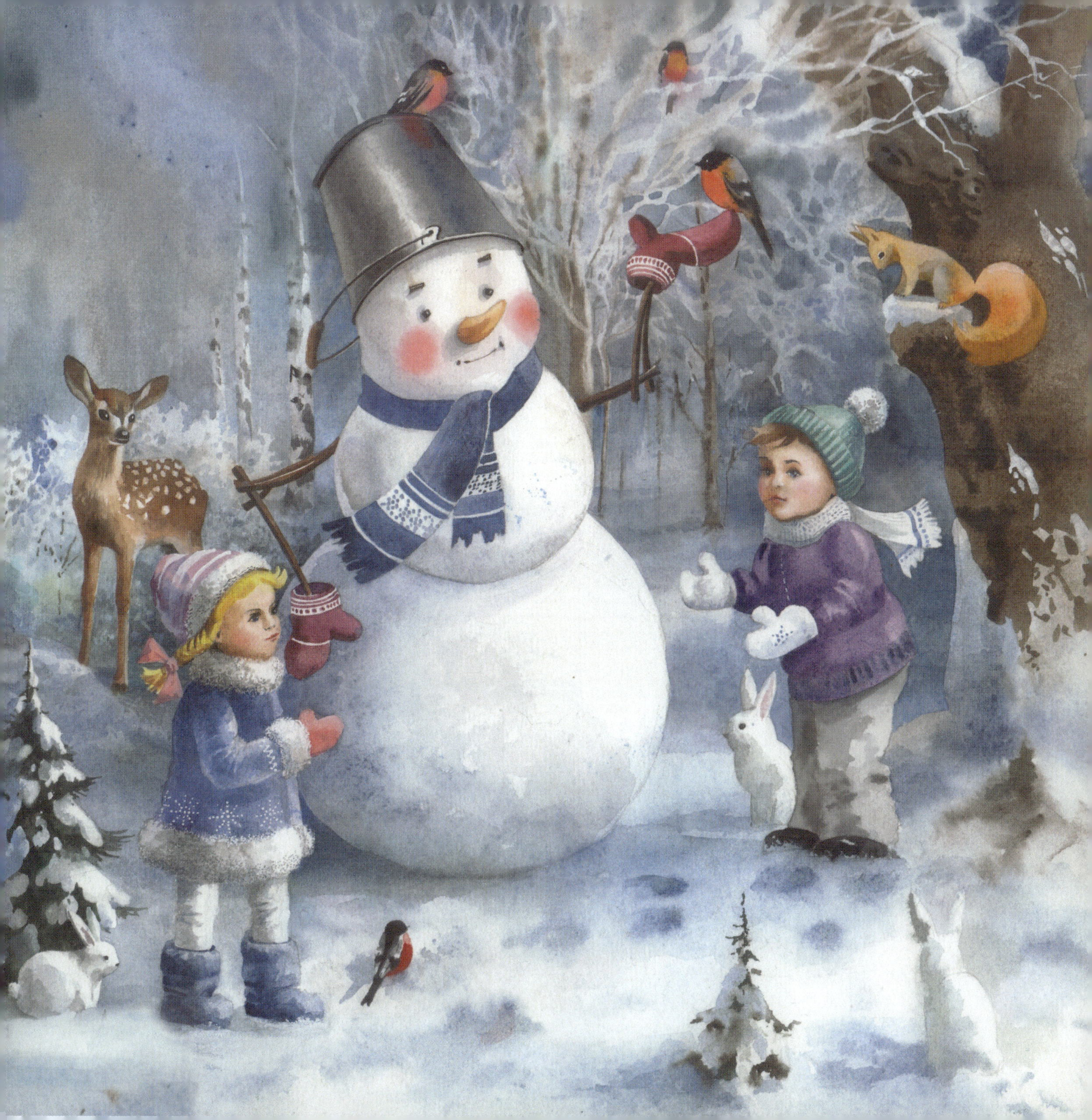

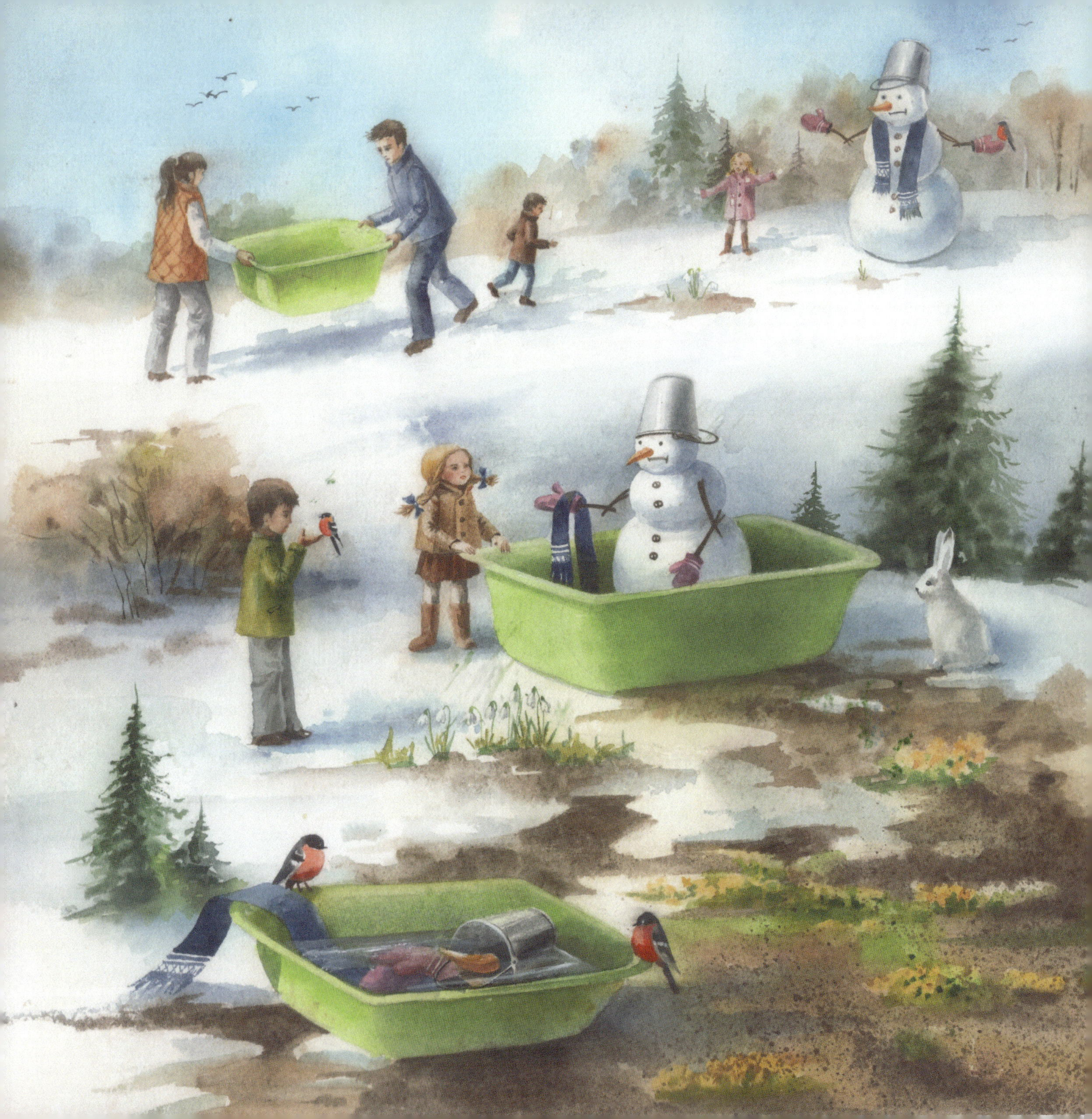

The whole winter passed in merry games with the snowman whom they named Jumpsy. They sledded and skied together but, more than anything else, the children loved being joined in their games by the forest animals.

Mum and Dad grew worried because they knew that, as soon as spring came, the snow would melt. They tried to prepare Holly for this in various ways, but Holly didn't even want to hear that something so terrible could happen. And, anyway, she assured them that she had a solution for that, if it ever happened.

As they had been afraid, with the first warm days Jumpsy began to melt, so Holly, with the help of her brother Thomas, fetched a large green tub and asked their parents to take it to the hill near the forest where Jumpsy spent his time in the company of lots of small wild animals.

The snowman did as he was told when they asked him to jump into the tub.

The next morning, the children were greeted by a tub full of water in which sat the old metal bucket and gloves while at the bottom were the buttons and a soaking wet scarf.

Although everyone knew that something like this could happen, they did not expect that this would actually happen, as he was special.

The children decided to keep the water until the following winter.

The seasons changed and, as happens every year, winter came back and, with the first low temperatures, the water they had faithfully kept and watched over all this time froze.

'And what are we going to do now?' said Holly, absolutely terrified by the thought of not being able to build him again. 'It was to be expected that the water would transform him into ice and not flakes of snow,' Elizabeth said, a little annoyed. 'Well, we can't re-make a snowman out of ice,' Thomas added. 'But we can melt it and use the snow cannon* on the ski runs to make snowflakes,' Joseph, the eldest brother, said.

After agreeing that this was the best solution, the youngsters asked their parents for help. They melted the ice and connected the water to the snow cannon. When snowflakes started coming out of the barrel, the children caught them with buckets and in this way managed to pick up all the flakes that came out of it.

They brought the snow to the front of their house and made it into a snowman. They put the old metal bucket and the same black buttons, gloves and scarf on him. Mum got a new carrot and Dad added two round lumps of coal. Although he was the same, Jumpsy did not move.

The children felt bereft. Dad hugged them and Mum tried to comfort them with her words. 'You tried! That is the most important thing, isn't it?' 'But we did everything the same as the first time!' The children were genuinely saddened.

* See the end of the story under 'Fun Facts'.

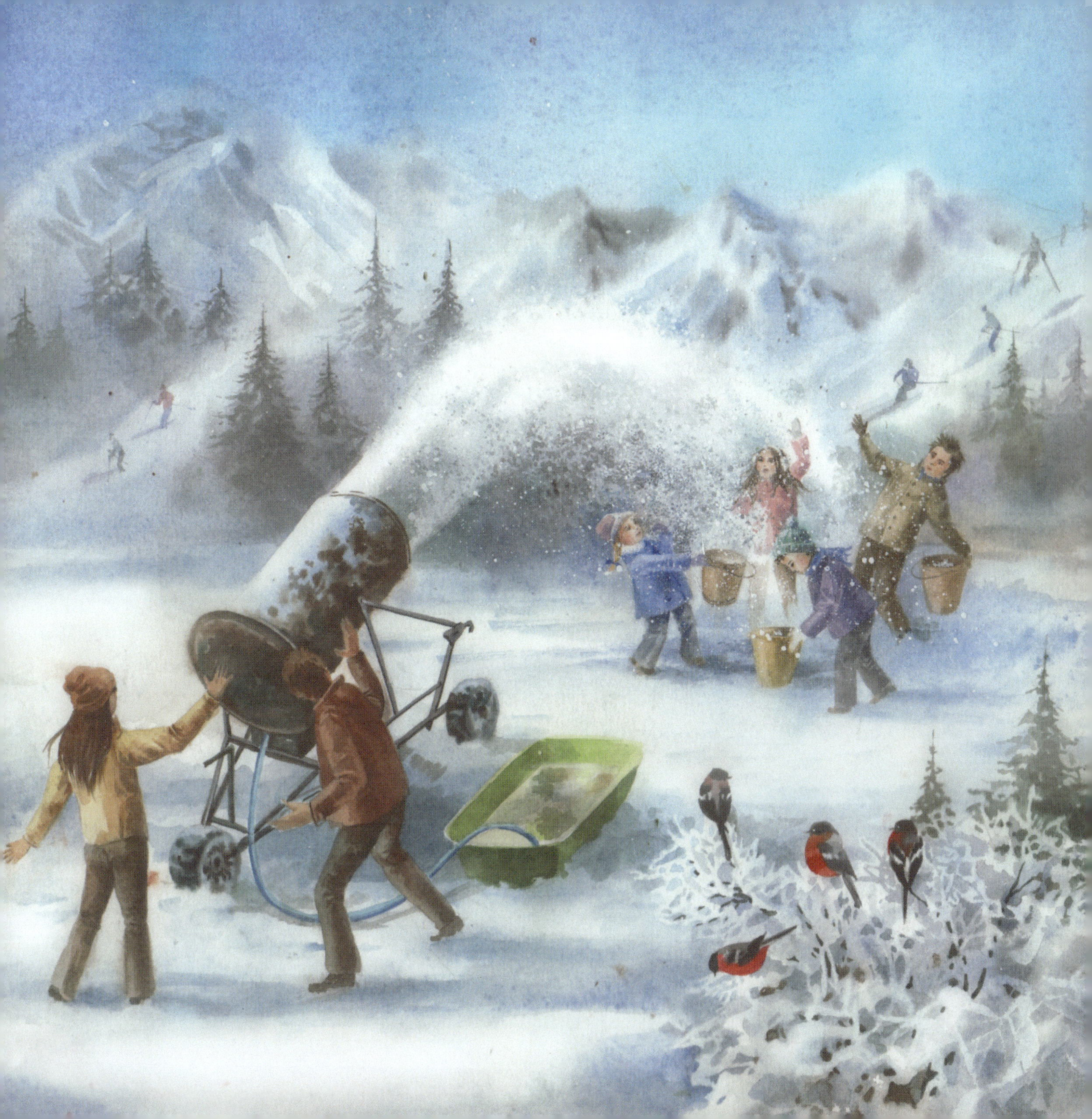

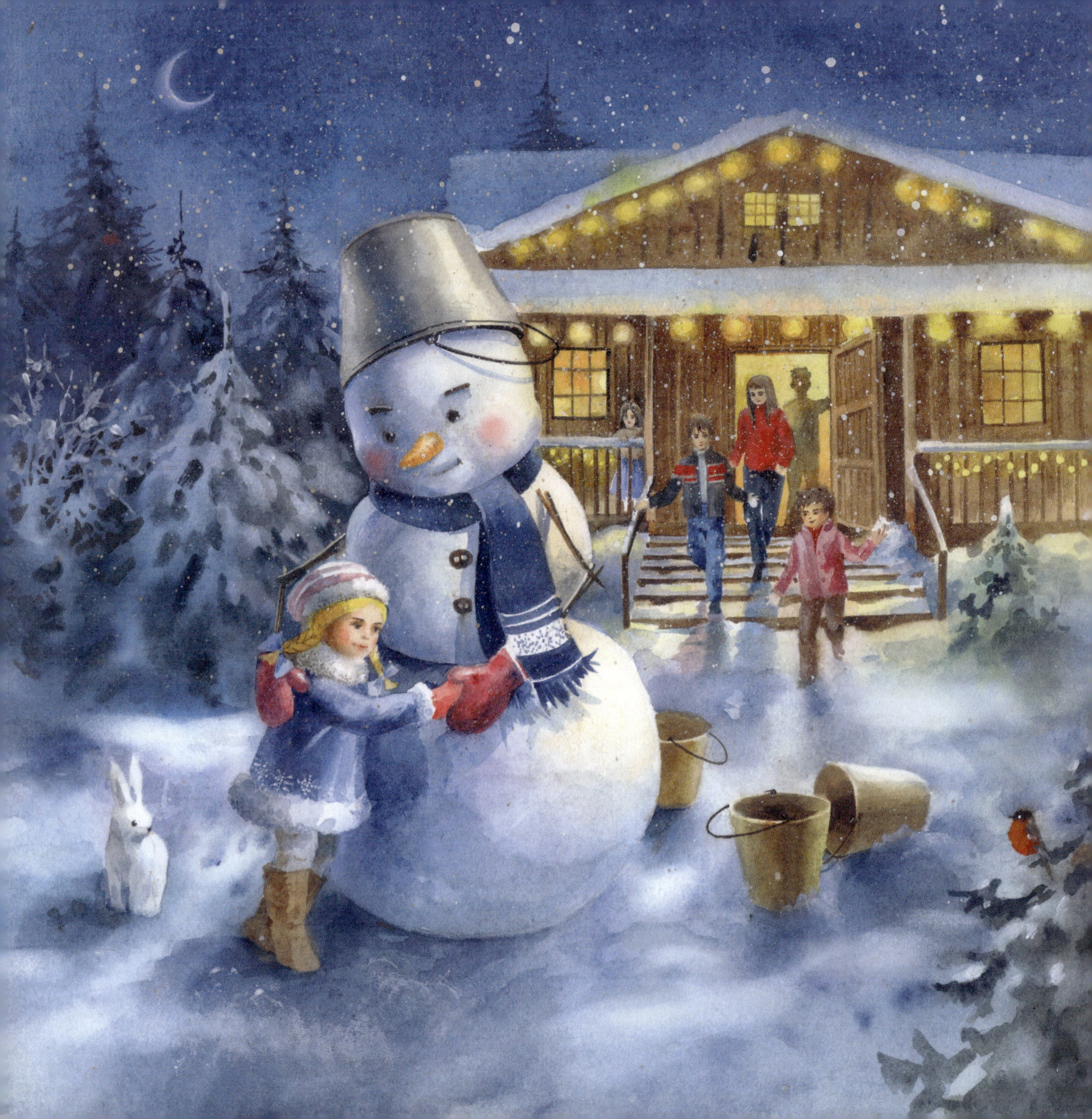

'Holly, let's go home,' said Thomas, after the others had left for the warmth of the house. 'No, I'll wait a bit longer,' the little girl replied. 'All right then,' said her brother, deciding to join the others.

At last, Holly decided it was time to accept that the snowman would not come to life like last Christmas. She stepped up to hug and kiss him while saying 'It's nice meeting you,' before turning away from her snowy friend to head into the house.

Then, she heard a familiar voice calling her name. Startled, Holly turned and luckily Jumpsy smiled at her, making her yell just as loud as she could. 'Dad! Mum! Everybody! Come quickly!'

They all flew out of the house and hugged their friend with general merriment. 'We did it!' Thomas shouted. 'We didn't doubt for a second,' Dad and Mum added happily, as they had also hoped in their hearts that they would see him again.

After they had exchanged hugs, Jumpsy cheerfully asked, 'And what did you all do while I was gone?' Holly answered, 'We have so much to tell you!'

The children outdid each other in recounting all the events that had happened to them during the whole year. Jumpsy laughed with them heartily, rejoicing along with his friends.

Fun Facts

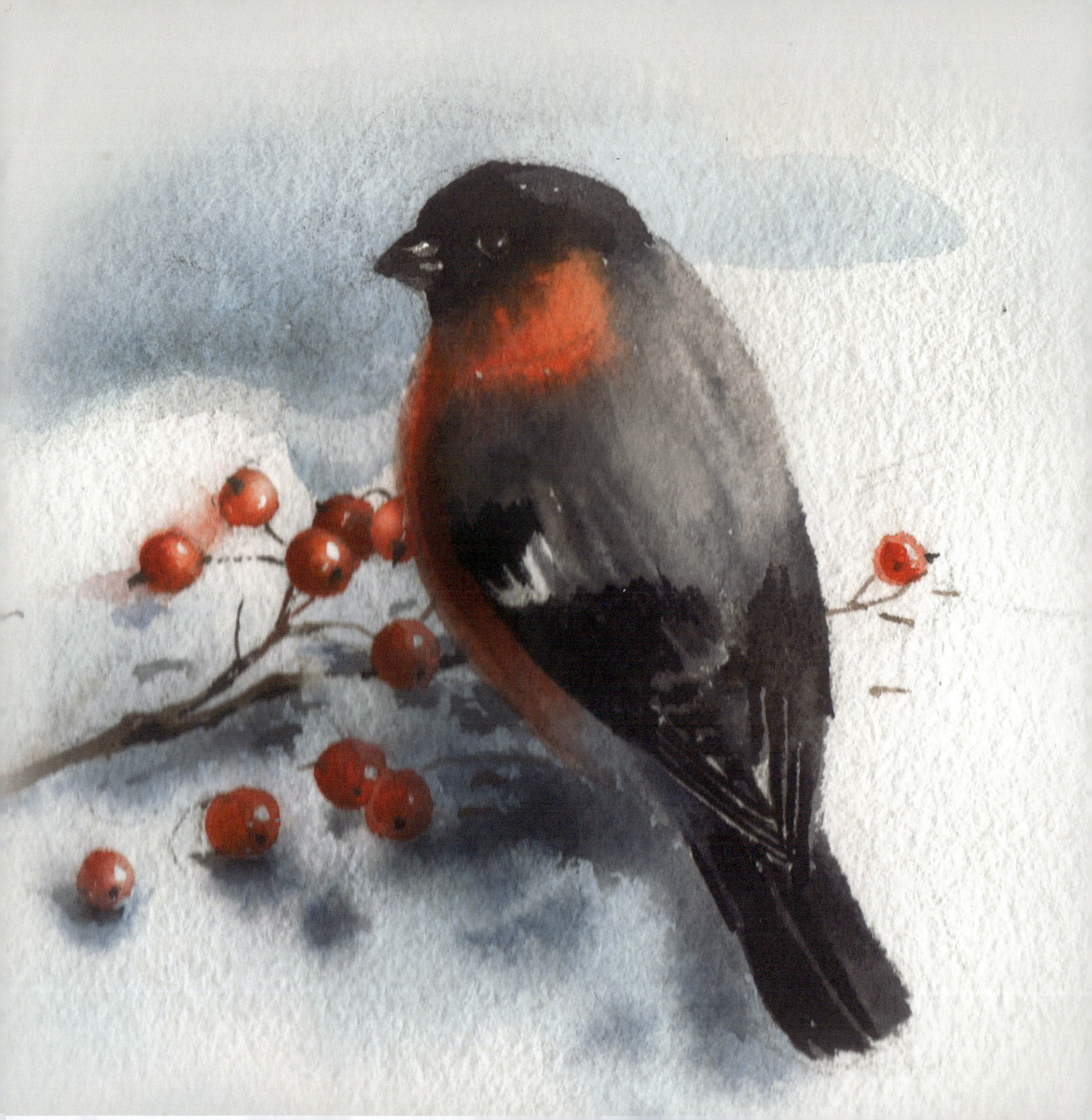

The Eurasian bullfinch

The Eurasian bullfinch is a very striking bird, with a black cap on its head and, in the male, gorgeously vivid, dark red feathers on its cheeks and chest (the females are a little plainer, with the same black cap but lighter pink chest feathers). But, despite their colours, they can be quite shy and a little hard to find.

Like the European robin, which often features in our Christmas celebrations, most bullfinches are about the size of a sparrow, so they're not very big although they are very solidly built and have a strong bill built for cracking open seeds. And they are full of life! However, they don't have much of a song, whistling a simple, slightly wheezy, but quite charming, call when they communicate with each other through the dense hedges where they live.

In the spring, they love to eat the flower buds of fruit trees, and this has got them into a lot of trouble in the past with farmers. Otherwise, they are happy eating berries, soft fruits and of course seeds. When they are feeding their young, they develop pouches in their mouths to help them carry food back to their nests.

The lovely thing about bullfinches is that they pair up for life, unlike a lot of other birds. And so, where you do see them, you'll often see the male and the female together, as a couple. Not one without the other.

Hares

Hares are funny creatures that are not that small at all. They can grow up to 5 kg (11 lb). Their body length can stretch to 75 cm (31 in) and their tail can be as long as 11 cm (4.3 in). A hare is bigger than a cat. They have long, muscular hind legs and short front legs. Hares can bound at speeds of up to 40 miles an hour, relying on their momentum and their ability to change direction at speed when running from danger. They have long ears and large protruding eyes placed on the sides of their head, giving them panoramic vision to help detect predators. They can even see above their heads.

Contrary to popular belief, not all rabbits change their fur in the winter. European hares keep the same colour throughout the year, while the Snowshoe, Arctic and Mountain Hare change their colour from brown or grey to white. They do this to blend in better with their winter environment, often digging shelter burrows in the snow. The tips of their ears remain darker and this is the only part that reveals them under the cover of snow.

In spring, hares fight with each other in a boxing match, standing on their hind legs and slapping each other with their forelegs. It was thought that these struggles were left only to male hares, but it is now known that the participants are often females defending themselves from the attention of males.

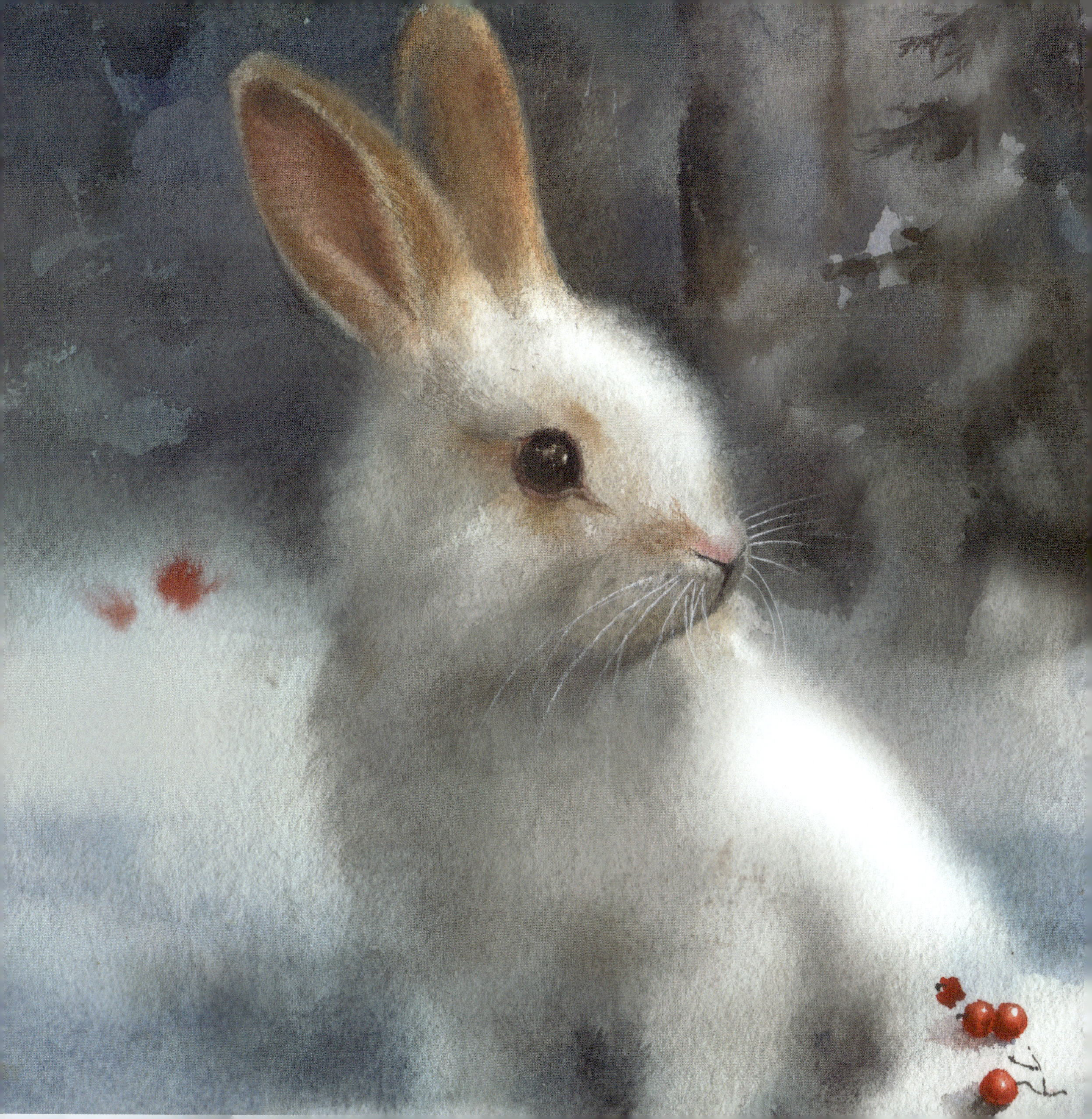

Snow Cannon

The first snowmaking machine was invented in 1934. It was meant for the company requirements of Warner Bros, but sometimes they used it for ceremonies and special events.

Many years passed before the first snow cannon was invented as we know it today. This was first used in 1952. Snowmaking was not used extensively until the 1970s. Today, however, many ski resorts depend heavily on snow cannons as there is not as much snow in so many of them.

The exciting thing is that they use water and icy air blown through the tube to make snow. Previously the quality of the snow depended on the knowledge of the person who was behind the cannon but, today, everything is controlled by computers.

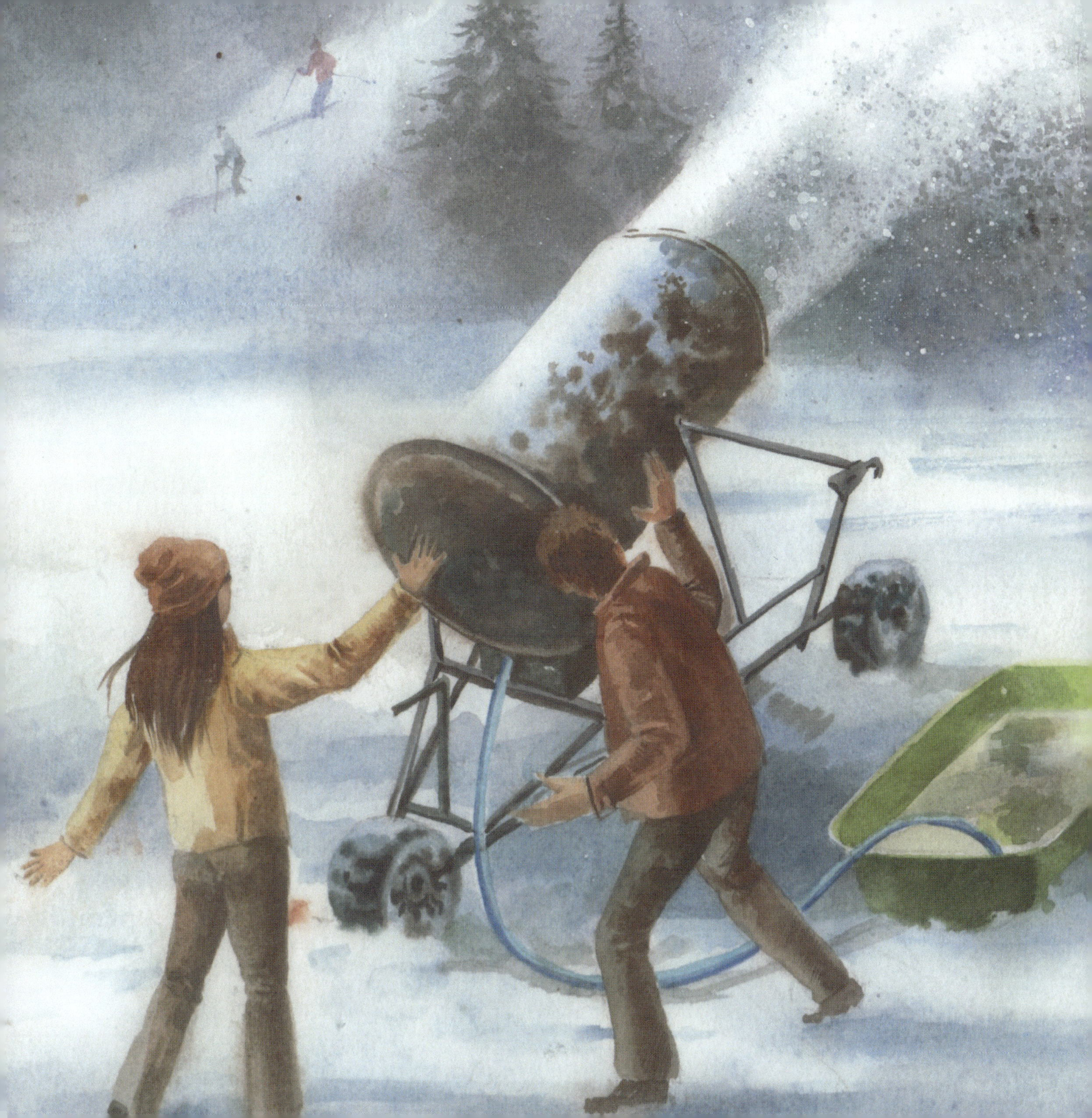

About the Illustrator

Besedina Anastasia was born in Moscow, Russia.

From an early age she loved art and as result she graduated from Moscow Art College of Applied Arts, with a degree in art painting.

Her great love is to paint everything about nature while creating portraits also gives her great pleasure. Besides this, she takes every opportunity to make illustrations for books like this one.

About the Author

Sanja Mach was born in Split, Croatia on 6 June 1980. She graduated from the University of Split with a degree in Economics. Sanja is Mum to Frane (13) and Anja (9) who are the very reason she discovered creative writing and her love of storytelling.

She writes fiction and stories for children.

This is her sixth story published on Amazon.

In addition to this, she also wrote 'Curious Gecko', 'Emma', 'The Crowd in the Ocean' serial and 'Who is Hope?'.

Some of her books are available in other languages.

The End

Printed in Great Britain
by Amazon